BASS
RECORDED VERSIONS
AUTHENTIC TRANSCRIPTIONS
WITH NOTES & TABLATURE
Transcribed by
JEFF HOLCK

Pink Floyd
Dark Side Of The Moon

T0045376

ISBN 978-0-7935-0420-6

7777 W. BLUEMOUND RD. P.O. BOX 13819 MILWAUKEE, WI 53213

Pink Floyd
Dark Side Of The Moon

Contents

BASS NOTATION LEGEND

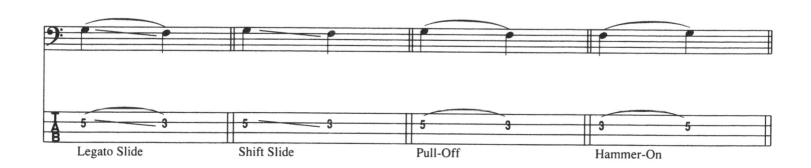

Legato Slide   Shift Slide   Pull-Off   Hammer-On

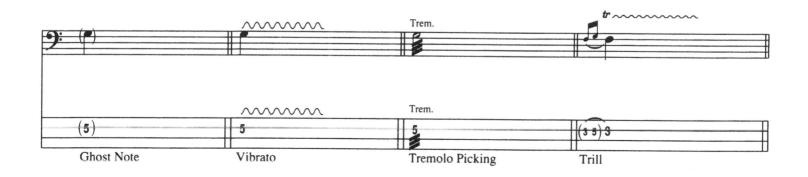

Ghost Note   Vibrato   Tremolo Picking   Trill

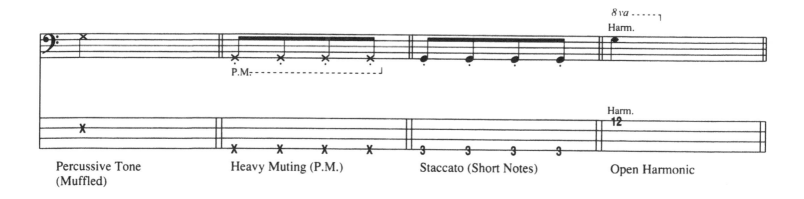

Percussive Tone (Muffled)   Heavy Muting (P.M.)   Staccato (Short Notes)   Open Harmonic

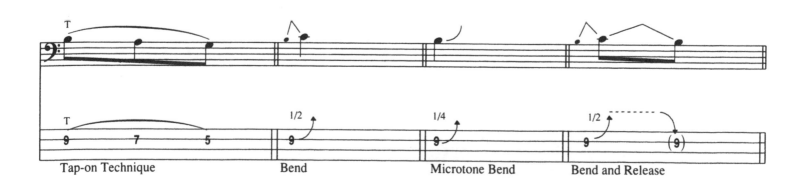

Tap-on Technique   Bend   Microtone Bend   Bend and Release

Breathe

Words by Roger Waters
Music by Roger Waters, David Gilmour & Rick Wright

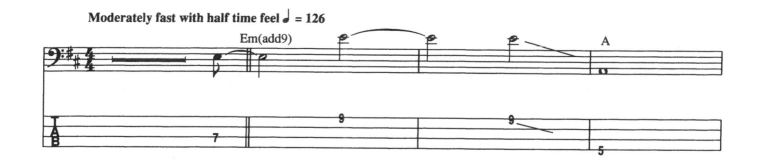

long you live,_ and high you fly, and smiles you'll give,_ and tears_ you'll cry.

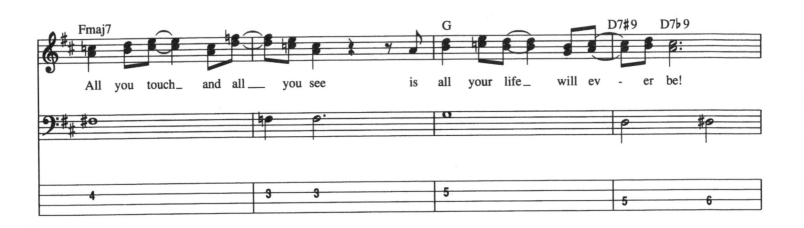

All you touch_ and all __ you see is all your life_ will ev - er be!

Run,_ rab - bit, run!_

Dig that hole, _____ for - get _ the sun. _____

Time

Words and Music by Roger Waters, Nicholas Mason, David Gilmour and Rick Wright

Intro
Moderately with half time feel ♩ = 128

with clocks, alarms, and   N.C.(E)
bells for approximately 40 seconds

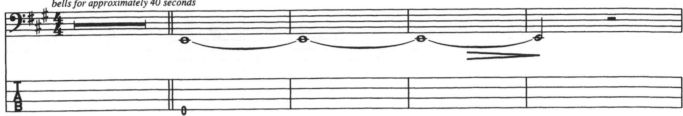

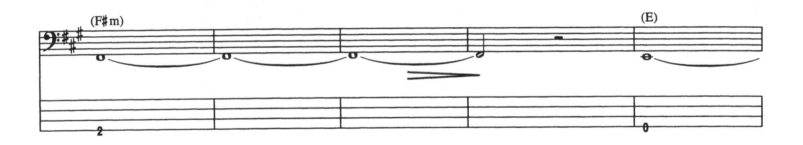

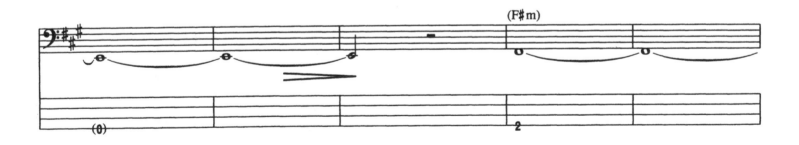

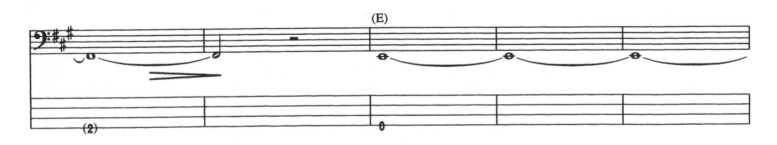

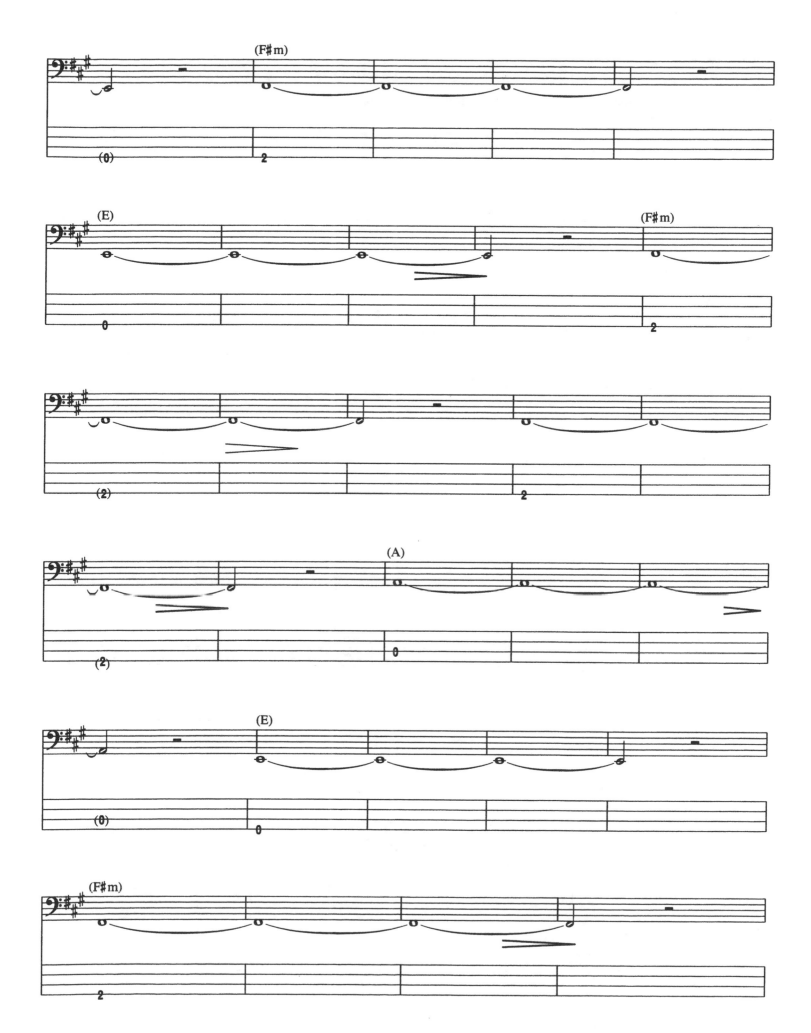

Wait - ing for some - one or some - thing to show __ you the way. ____

Tired of ly - ing in ____ the sun - shine.

Stay - ing home __ to watch __ the rain, And you are young and life __

__ is long, __ And there is time to kill ____ to - day.

15

And then one day you find __ Ten years have got __ be - hind __ you.

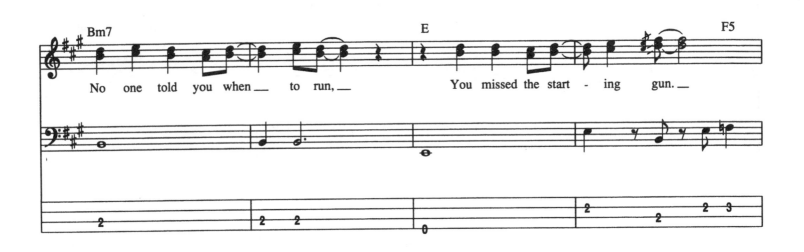

No one told you when __ to run, __ You missed the start - ing gun. __

Guitar Solo

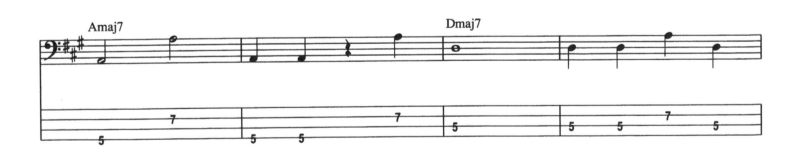

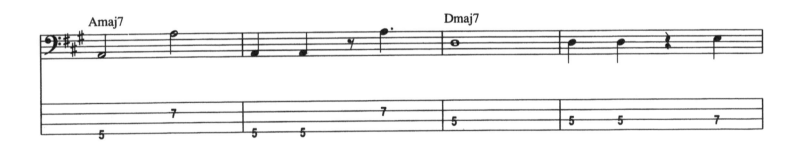

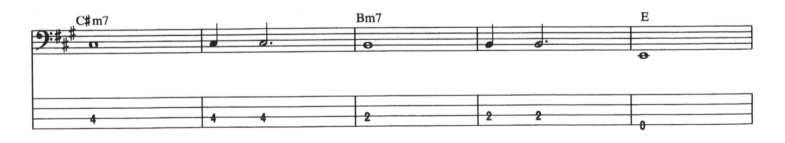

scrib - bled lines. Hang - ing on in quiet des - per - a - tion is the Eng - lish way. The time is gone, the song is o - ver. Thought I'd some - thing more to say.

Breathe (Reprise)

Words by Roger Waters
Music by Roger Waters, David Gilmour & Rick Wright

Moderately with half time feel ♩ = 122

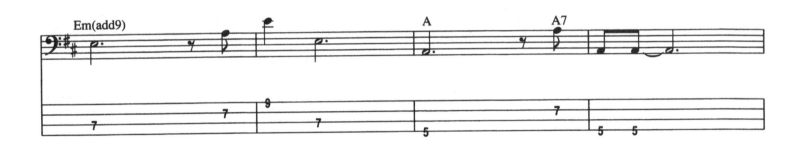

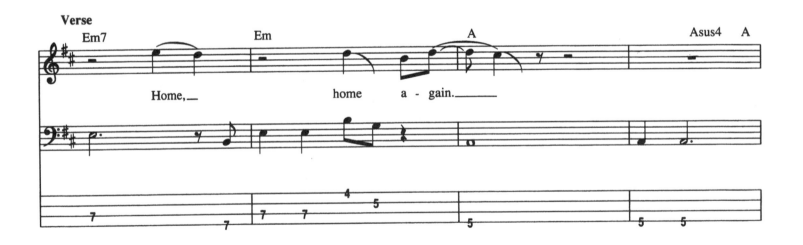

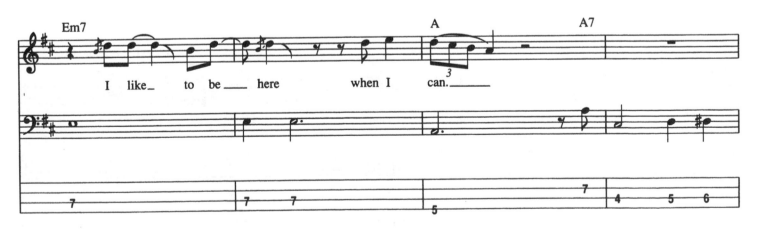

The Great Gig In The Sky

Words by Roger Waters; Music by Rick Wright

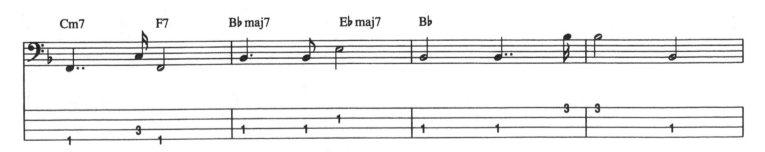

Vocal Scat Solo

Spoken: I never said I was afraid of dying.

Money

Words and Music by Roger Waters

F#m7

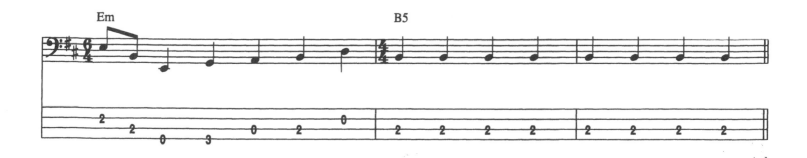

Em

B5

Guitar Solo 1

B5

Em

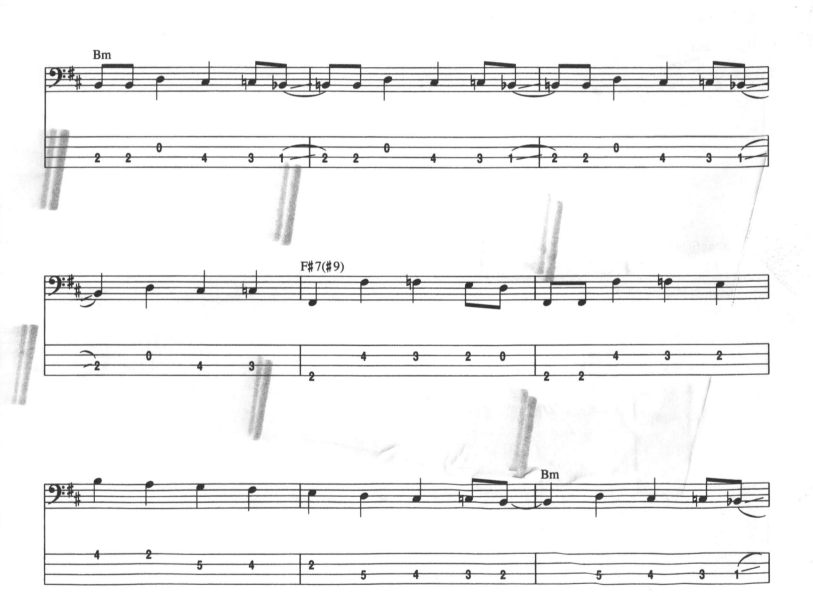

Guitar Solo 3

way,_____ a - way,_____ a - way,_____ a - way,_

_____ a - way,_____ a - way,_____ a - way,_

_____ a - way,_____ Woo!_____

vocal ad lib simile with
background conversation effects

Us And Them

Words by Roger Waters
Music by Roger Waters & Rick Wright

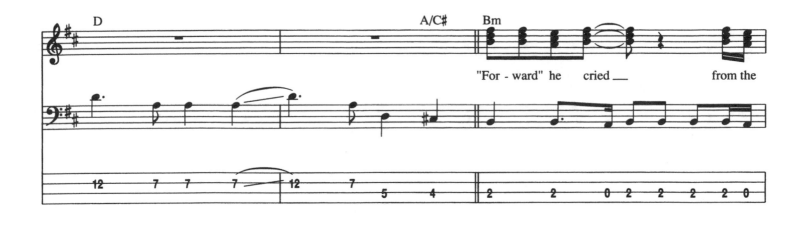

"For - ward" he cried ___ from the

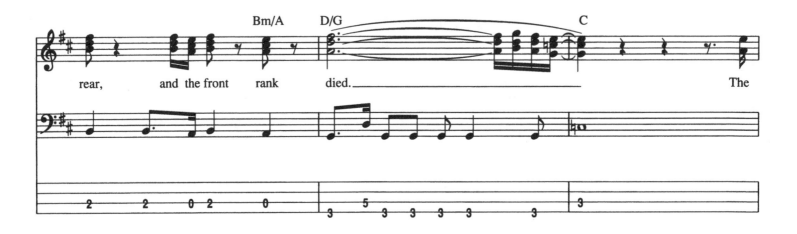

rear, and the front rank died. ___ The

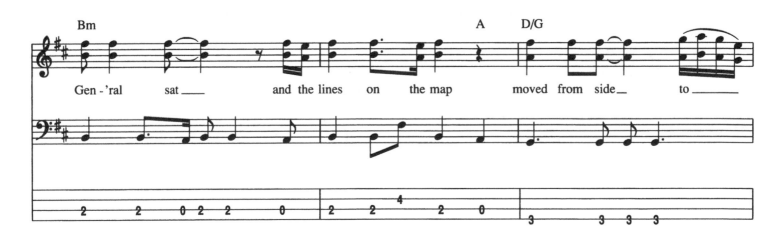

Gen -'ral sat ___ and the lines on the map moved from side ___ to ___

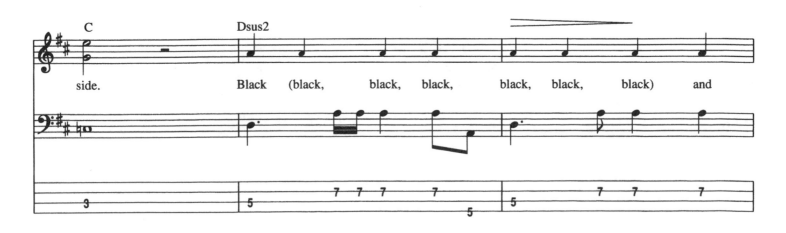

side. Black (black, black, black, black, black, black) and

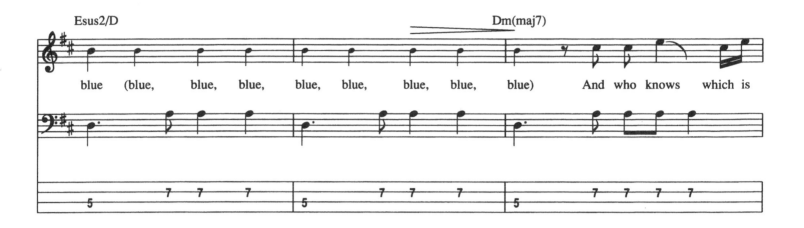

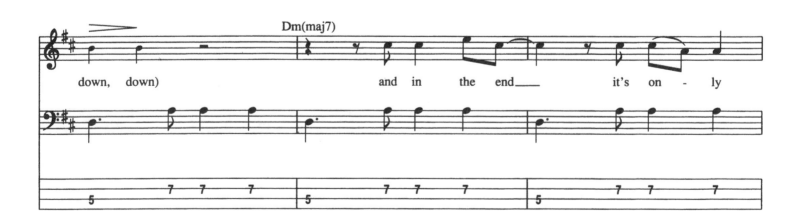

'round and 'round _ ('round, 'round) and 'round ('round, 'round, 'round)

"Have-n't you heard? _ It's a bat-tle of words," the

post - er bear - er _ cried. "Lis - ten, _ son," _ said the man _

_ with the gun, _ "There's room for you _ in - side."

44

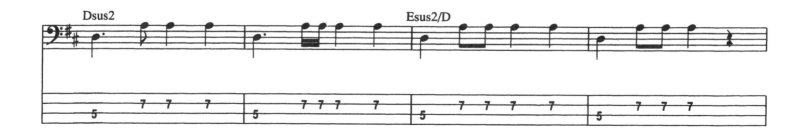

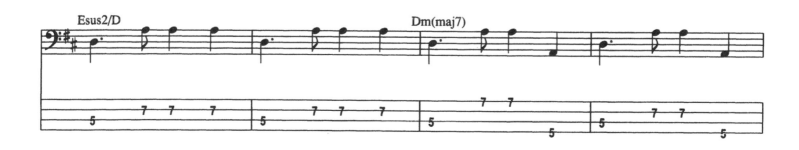

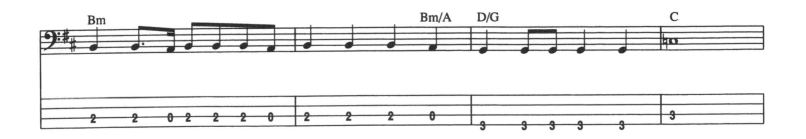

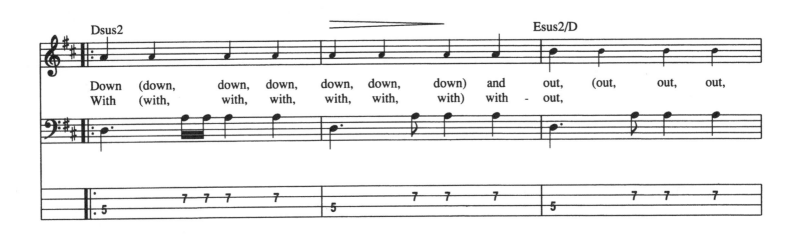

Down (down, down, down, down, down, down) and out, (out, out, out,
With (with, with, with, with, with, with) with - out,

out, out, out, out)   It can't be helped __ but there's __ a
                                        And who'll de - ny ___   it's what __ the

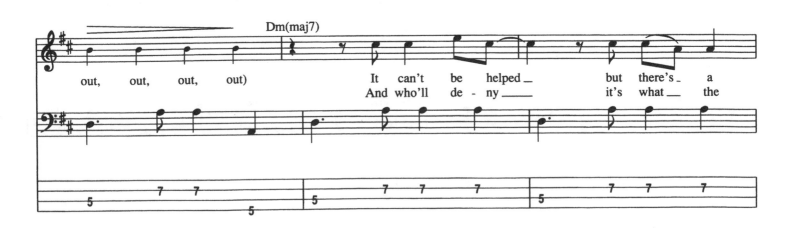

Breathe (Second Reprise)

Words by Roger Waters
Music by Roger Waters, David Gilmour & Rick Wright

Moderately slow with half time feel ♩ = 73

Brain Damage

Words and Music by Roger Waters

Intro
Moderately fast with half time feel ♩ = 131

Verse

The lu - na - tic ___ is on the grass. ___

The lu - na - tic ___ is on the grass, ___

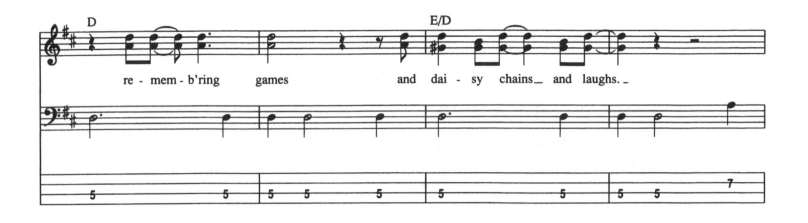

re - mem - b'ring games and dai - sy chains__ and laughs.__

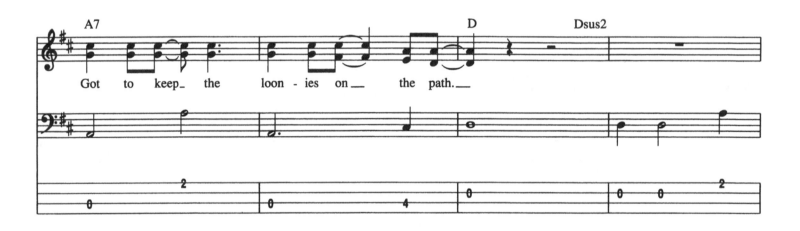

Got to keep__ the loon - ies on __ the path.__

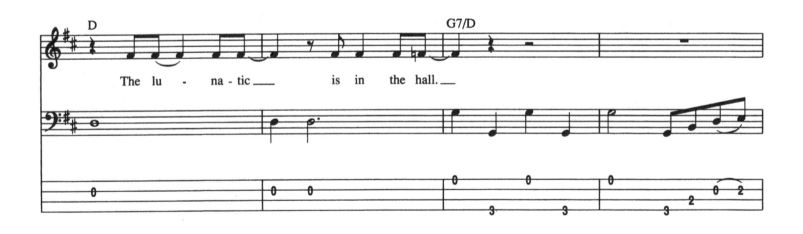

The lu - na - tic__ is in the hall.__

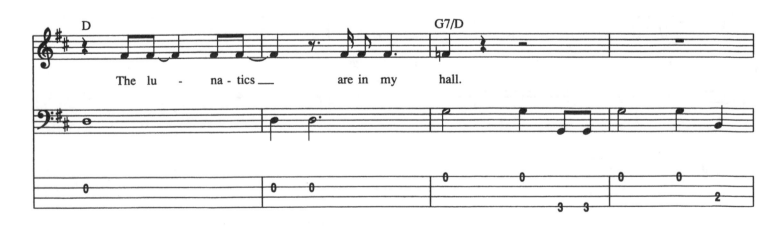

The lu - na - tics__ are in my hall.

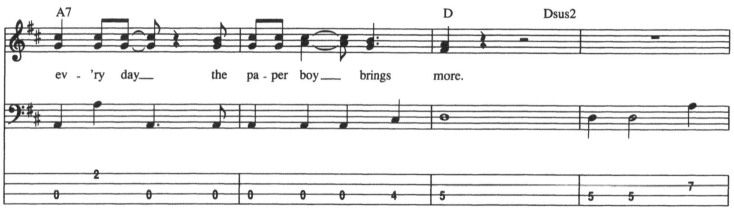

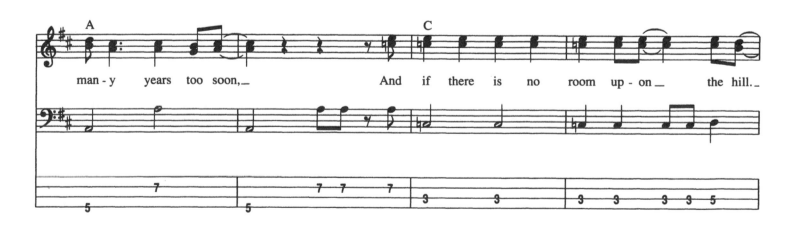

The lu - na - tic ____ is in my head. ____

You raise ____ the blade, ____ you make ____ the change. ____

You re - ar - range ____ me till I'm sane. ____

You lock the door, ____ and throw a - way ____ the key. ____ There's

some-one in my head, but it's not me.

And if the cloud __ bursts thun - der in __ your ear, __ you shout __ and no - one seems to hear. __

And if the band __ you're in __ starts

play - in' dif - f'rent tunes, ___ I'll see you on the dark ___ side ___ of the moon. ___

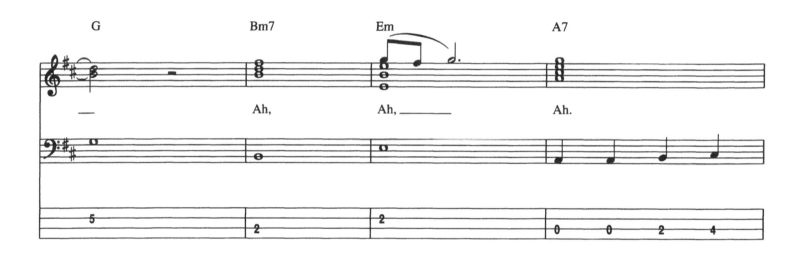

___ Ah, Ah, _____ Ah.

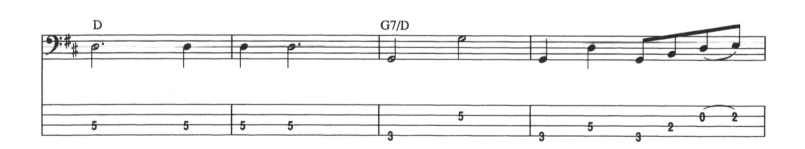

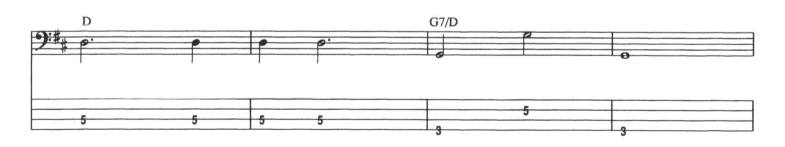

Segue to "Eclipse"

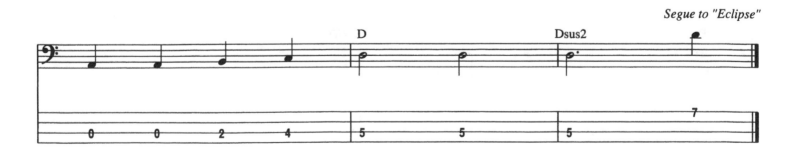

Eclipse

Words and Music by Roger Waters

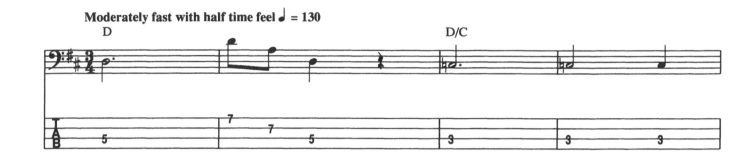

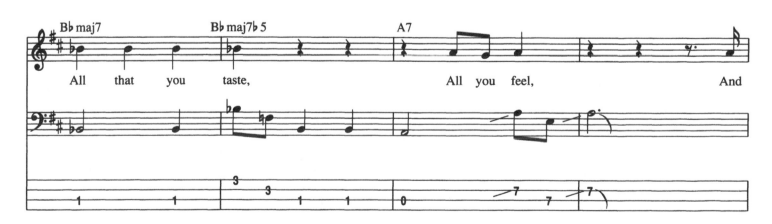

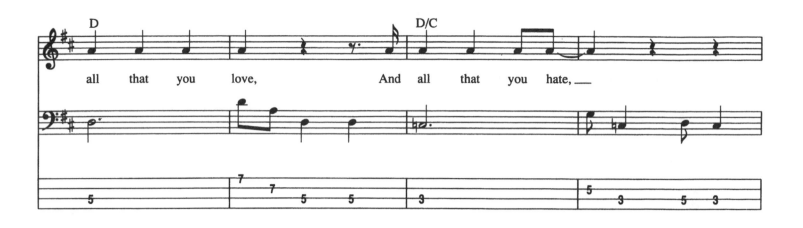

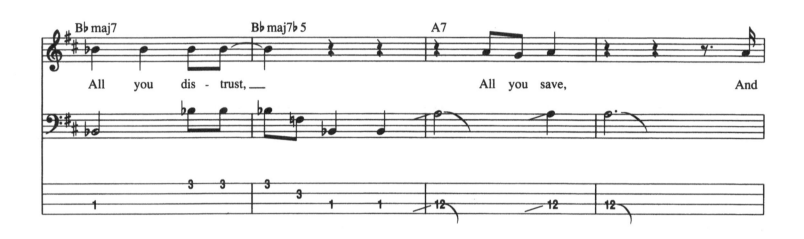

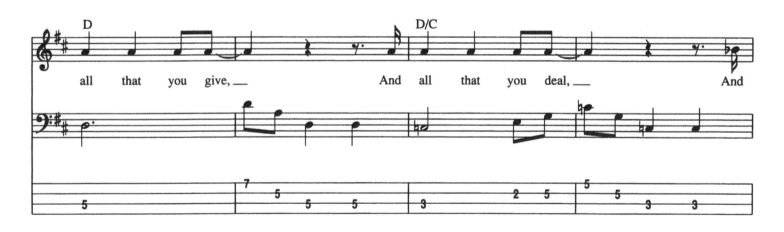

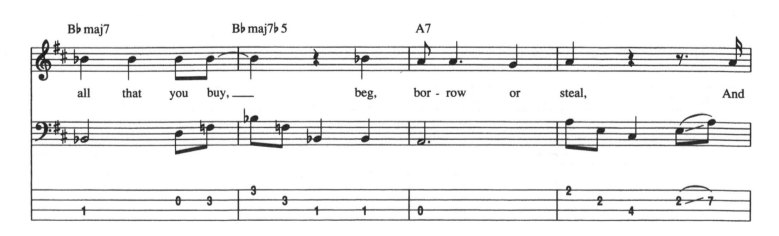

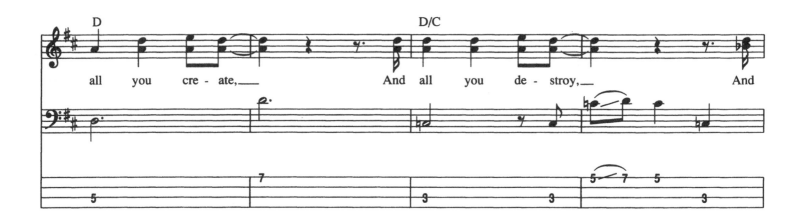

all you cre-ate,___ And all you de-stroy,___ And

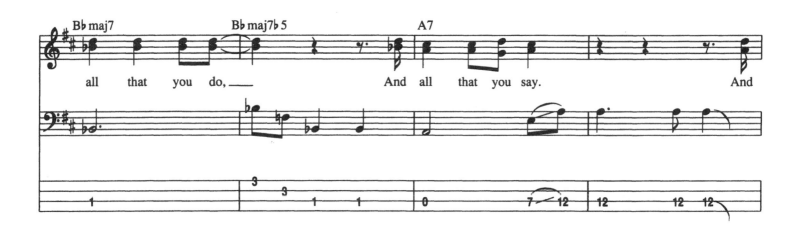

all that you do,___ And all that you say. And

all that you eat.___ And ev-'ry one you meet, And

all that you slight,___ And ev-'ry one you fight. And

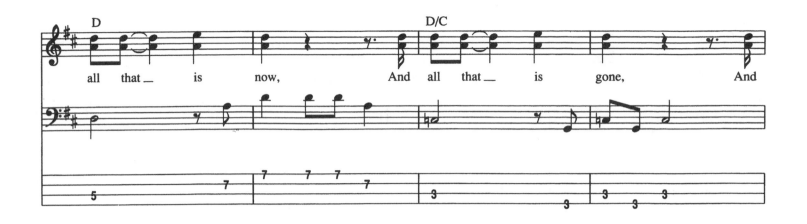

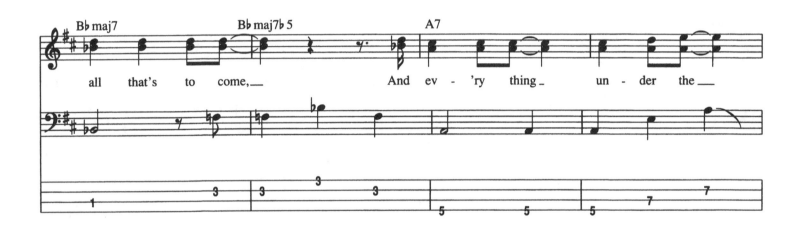

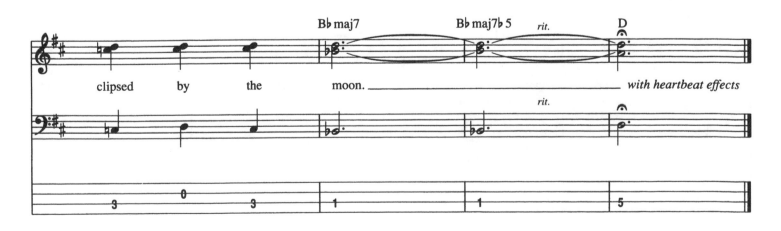

BASS RECORDED VERSIONS

Bass Recorded Versions feature authentic transcriptions written in standard notation and tablature for bass guitar. This series features complete bass lines from the classics to contemporary superstars.

25 Essential Rock Bass Classics
00690210 / $19.99

Avenged Sevenfold – Nightmare
00691054 / $19.99

The Beatles – Abbey Road
00128336 / $24.99

The Beatles – 1962-1966
00690556 / $19.99

The Beatles – 1967-1970
00690557 / $24.99

Best of Bass Tab
00141806 / $17.99

The Best of Blink 182
00690549 / $18.99

Blues Bass Classics
00690291 / $22.99

Boston – Bass Collection
00690935 / $19.95

Stanley Clarke – Collection
00672307 / $22.99

Dream Theater – Bass Anthology
00119345 / $29.99

Funk Bass Bible
00690744 / $24.99

Hard Rock Bass Bible
00690746 / $22.99

Jimi Hendrix – Are You Experienced?
00690371 / $17.95

Jimi Hendrix – Bass Tab Collection
00160505 / $24.99

Iron Maiden – Bass Anthology
00690867 / $24.99

Jazz Bass Classics
00102070 / $19.99

The Best of Kiss
00690080 / $22.99

Lynyrd Skynyrd – All-Time Greatest Hits
00690956 / $24.99

Bob Marley – Bass Collection
00690568 / $24.99

Mastodon – Crack the Skye
00691007 / $19.99

Megadeth – Bass Anthology
00691191 / $22.99

Metal Bass Tabs
00103358 / $22.99

Best of Marcus Miller
00690811 / $24.99

Motown Bass Classics
00690253 / $19.99

Muse – Bass Tab Collection
00123275 / $22.99

Nirvana – Bass Collection
00690066 / $19.99

Nothing More – Guitar & Bass Collection
00265439 / $24.99

The Offspring – Greatest Hits
00690809 / $17.95

The Essential Jaco Pastorius
00690420 / $22.99

Jaco Pastorius – Greatest Jazz Fusion Bass Player
00690421 / $24.99

Pearl Jam – Ten
00694882 / $19.99

Pink Floyd – Dark Side of the Moon
00660172 / $17.99

The Best of Police
00660207 / $24.99

Pop/Rock Bass Bible
00690747 / $24.99

Queen – The Bass Collection
00690065 / $22.99

R&B Bass Bible
00690745 / $24.99

Rage Against the Machine
00690248 / $19.99

Red Hot Chili Peppers – BloodSugarSexMagik
00690064 / $19.99

Red Hot Chili Peppers – By the Way
00690585 / $24.99

Red Hot Chili Peppers – Californication
00690390 / $22.99

Red Hot Chili Peppers – Greatest Hits
00690675 / $22.99

Red Hot Chili Peppers – I'm with You
00691167 / $22.99

Red Hot Chili Peppers – One Hot Minute
00690091 / $22.99

Red Hot Chili Peppers – Stadium Arcadium
00690853 / Book Only $24.95

Rock Bass Bible
00690446 / $22.99

Rolling Stones – Bass Collection
00690256 / $24.99

Royal Blood
00151826 / $24.99

Rush – The Spirit of Radio: Greatest Hits 1974-1987
00323856 / $24.99

Best of Billy Sheehan
00173972 / $24.99

Slap Bass Bible
00159716 / $29.99

Sly & The Family Stone for Bass
00109733 / $22.99

Best of Yes
00103044 / $24.99

Best of ZZ Top for Bass
00691069 / $24.99